Heaven Starts Here

Heaven Starts Here

A GUIDE TO END OF LIFE

YASMEEN FATIMAH, RN

Charleston, SC
www.PalmettoPublishing.com

Heaven Starts Here

Copyright © 2022 by Yasmeen Fatimah, RN

All rights reserved.

No portion of this book may be reproduced, stored in a retrieval system, or transmitted in any form by any means–electronic, mechanical, photocopy, recording, or other–except for brief quotations in printed reviews, without prior permission of the author.

First Edition

Paperback ISBN: 979-8-88590-050-8
eBook ISBN: 979-8-88590-051-5

In Loving Memory of My Mom.
Your unconditional love made me who I am today . . .

Table of Contents

Introduction · xi

Stages of Dying · 1

A Few Weeks · 3

A Week or So · 7

Days · 10

Hours · 13

Frequently Asked Questions · · · · · · · · · · · · · · · 19

Notes · 22

About the Author · 25

The kingdom of God is not coming with signs observed or with visible display . . . For the kingdom of God (Heaven) is among you.

*The Gospel of Luke

Introduction

There have been many books and articles written on the subject of Death and Dying. The purpose of this book is to be informative regarding that process, while also being enlightening and encouraging to those experiencing the dying process or has a loved one who is. We are all born, and surely, we will all die. It is the one thing that every being on this planet will inescapably experience. We will experience the death of someone we know and likely love, and we will experience our own death. The only exception to experiencing the death of a loved one is if we ourselves don't live long enough to experience it. My hope is that by the end of reading this, you will have a little more peace and hopefully some acceptance of the inevitable. To fully accept this realization is freedom. Freedom from the worry of "Will I lose a loved one to death or if I will die?" The answer to that is already written. You know, this is a journey? I hope this helps.

YASMEEN FATIMAH, RN

Some of us will experience life-limiting illnesses personally or by way of someone close to us. If you are reading this, it is likely that you are in the midst of that very experience. Those of us that have had or are having those experiences have a general idea of the how death will occur, and some doctor has given his or her interpretation of the when death will occur. The only difference between someone with a life-limiting illness or a terminal disease and someone who is relatively healthy on this journey that ends the same for us all is that, that illness gives an idea of the how and when. Some of us will live long, full lives well into their eighties and nineties and some (very rarely) past hundred. You may be amongst those fortunate enough to experience your loved ones for decades. It is important to keep things in perspective when we have been blessed to experience long, full lives or have loved ones who have been blessed to live to see generations birthed after them. It is truly a privilege. I mean how many hundred-year-old's do you know?

***

When we are accepting of the things that we don't necessarily have control over—terminal illness and old age, for example—peace and freedom is unleashed. In the knowing that time is limited, we get to choose, in some cases, the where. Do I want to be in a cold hospital surrounded by noise and unfamiliarity? Or do I want to be in the place that makes me the happiest, surrounded by the people I love and that love me most.

Dying is much like being born, in that there are similarities that most all experience. Both processes can be outlined by the common symptoms that most everyone will encounter. Of course, each experience will have its own unique components. Like being born, dying is a natural process. Dying is meant to be. Before we get into the specifics of dying and what that may look like, let us talk about living, or what I like to refer to as Being. Being present in any and all circumstance is vital to a meaningful life. The present moment at any given time is all we have.

The past is gone, and tomorrow is simply the present in waiting. So often when sickness occurs, we completely forget about the present. We are caught up in whatever may have gone "wrong." We focus on doctors' appointments and treatments—what not to eat, what not to drink, what not to do. I see this often in the elderly population as well. Whether it is the actual person or loved ones. We are so caught up in fixing the thing that we perceive as broken. So much so that we often forget to just Be. Under any circumstance or stage in life, it is important to be intentional about moments.

We all have a finite amount of time in this realm. How much more important is it to take advantage of the knowing? The knowing that our finite time may be winding up. I know that doctors are not always forthcoming when it comes to terminal diagnoses and treatments. I also know that even when doctors are forthcoming, patients and families are not always receptive to the news. I understand the magnitude of the devastation of hearing the news that your loved one is dying, whether one is given five years, five months, or five days. Hearing a definitive time frame on life hits a proverbial stopwatch and it is almost impossible to take our eyes off it once it starts. What if we shifted our focus? What if instead of focusing on Fixing or what not to do, we focused on Being. Being present, being in the moment, being Love. The most unfortunate part of a doctor not being forthcoming or a patient and loved ones not being accepting of the inevitable is the denial. The denial causes to refuse all involved of the present moment.

***

HEAVEN STARTS HERE

*My mother passed away four years ago on July 7, 2017. She passed away at a hospice facility two weeks after a COPD exacerbation. I learned that my mother had COPD for almost three years before she passed. She had had it for some time prior to her diagnosis. It became more evident that there was something going on with her when I would speak to her on the phone, and she would be short of breath. Of course, being a nurse and a hospice nurse to boot, I did not need much more than a confirmation from the pulmonologist. I remember how annoyed she was when she got her oxygen. She did not want to wear it. She didn't think she needed it. I remember going to one of her appointments and telling the doctor about her refusal. He said to her in that appointment, "Your disease is not reversible, and the oxygen right now is the only thing prolonging your life." I don't know if she heard him or was receptive at all. We battled about the oxygen for a little while longer. What I do know is that I heard him. I made it a point from that moment forward to be intentional about celebrating her, to be intentional about being present. Not every day was a party. Some days it looked like me lying across her bed, soaking up her essence. Every birthday was a big deal, though. I invited everyone I knew she would want to see and that wanted to see her. She had no idea why I made it a point to make it a big deal and neither did any of them. The first couple of birthday parties we had, she refused to wear her oxygen. She didn't want it on in the pictures. Her refusing to wear her oxygen didn't matter, all that mattered was that she was happy and smiling. On her last birthday we celebrated, she was wearing her oxygen. She has it on in all the pictures, and it didn't matter to her because we had our moment. There was oxygen in the picture but there were also smiles. I am grateful for the knowing the intuition and awareness of the fragility of life. I am grateful that in the knowing, I was able to be in the moment. I feel my mom's presence often, I don't have the answers about what happens when our spirit leaves our bodies, but I do know that I was able to experience Heaven with her right here, and I am forever grateful for that.

It is completely normal to be anxious, nervous, and completely terrified while experiencing the dying process. A lot of people are experiencing the loss of a loved one for the first time. If you are the person facing death, this is definitely your first time. It is often said that we only live once, yes? However, we have an opportunity to live every day we wake up. There is something to be grateful for, even if you know that today is the day. In all honesty, wouldn't knowing today could be the day make it even more precious? I think knowing what is happening and what to expect, while it does not eliminate the pain of what is going on, does allow a wonderful opportunity—opportunity to be fully in the moment as often as possible. Being aware of some common signs and symptoms of dying allows for some sense of peace with the process. The next few pages will explain some of what you may experience or see leading up to death.

Stages of Dying

A few months before a person dies, you may notice them being a little more withdrawn. There won't likely be much interest in visitors or talking on the phone. You may notice there is some increased weakness. Specific symptoms differ depending on the illness, but one being increasingly tired is pretty common across the board. Their sleep increases. These symptoms are attributed to the realization of im-\pending death. If the person is lucid and aware of what is going on, you can imagine that this part of the journey may be anxiety producing. While sleep has increased, one may still need medication to help them stay asleep at night. This is when the mind is racing, and surroundings are typically most quiet, so thoughts are the loudest.

* * *

It is important that we talk to our loved one and do the things that bring them the most comfort and joy, whatever that might be. Now is not the time to hound them about what they should or should not eat or drink. It is also important not to push them for engagement. When you're having a difficult day or don't feel well, you likely want to be left alone, at least for a little while. It's ok and completely normal.

It is likely that you have already had a conversation with your loved one on what they desire. Perhaps a few doctors and nurses have asked questions pertaining to the subject. Hospice services may have already been implemented in the care plan at this point, or there may have been talks about it. If we haven't had a conversation about what our loved one's desires are, now is a good time to do so. It's difficult, but remember, there's peace in knowing.

***

A Few Weeks

A few weeks before a person dies, their appetite will likely change. They may not want to eat as much if anything. Meals may be reduced to bites and sips. Once appetite and elimination slow down, many people ask the questions: Is my loved one starving to death? Shouldn't they have some fluids or even tube feeding? I can say from a clinical standpoint they are not starving. As mentioned in the previous paragraph, it is important to know your loved one's wishes as it relates to End of Life while they are able to express it. It is so important that we have these conversations even while we are healthy. It cuts down on confusion if and when the time comes to make tough decisions related to one's health when they aren't able to do it for themselves. It also provides the peace that comes from Knowing. In having these conversations in advance, one knows what to do and what is desired. Now during this time, the focus can be on love and support and being in the moment.

That being said, the gastrointestinal system is the first to slow as the body is overcompensating for the more vital systems during this process. Our body has energy storage and one can live off that storage for a couple of weeks without eating. Of course, we need water more frequently. Keep in mind that at this stage, the functioning of the body is slowing so none of these needs are equivalent to what an active individual would be. Forcing foods and liquids during this time can actually cause more harm than good. Forcing foods and liquids by mouth can cause choking and aspiration, leading to discomfort. Giving fluids and tube feeding during this time may also be harmful. A slowing gastrointestinal system is not going to be able to metabolize fluids being pumped in artificially as efficiently as it would in a healthy body. Therefore, those fluids will begin to seep into other places in the body, like tissues and lungs, causing fluid overload, swelling, and coughing. All of which can be very uncomfortable. This is why your doctors or hospice nurses may suggest the reduction or even discontinuation of tube feeding during this time; even in one that has been receiving these therapies long term.

It is not to hasten death but, rather, decrease those factors that may cause distress. One may become weaker and not even be able to get out of bed to do the things that they were able to do just a few days earlier. It's important during this time to focus on the things that will provide the most peace and comfort to your loved one. If your loved one is able to communicate, listen. Make those sips and bites count. If chocolate ice cream or a sip of Coke puts a smile on their face and provides some happiness, give it to them. Keep things in perspective. When we are denying our sick or elderly loved ones the simple pleasures of things they may want, what is the purpose? What is our goal? Are we afraid it may kill them? When one is dying, those little things don't matter.

***

YASMEEN FATIMAH, RN

*My mother loved turkey wings. She particularly liked them from Wyatt's Country barbeque. When she was too sick to really go out, I would try to get her a plate at least once a week if they didn't run out. That's just how good they are. About a week or so before my mother passed, a friend was coming to see her and check on me. My friend knew how much my mother loved these Turkey Wings, so she brought her a plate. Admittedly at the time, I was a bit annoyed. "She can't eat that, she can't even breathe," I told my friend. But I vividly remember my mother waking up and being elated, breathless and all about those Turkey Wings. She ate a good bit of them, too. I don't think she had really eaten a whole lot up to that point. Those Turkey Wings made her happy. Seeing her happy made me happy. That was a great moment. A little piece of heaven for her and me.

***

A Week or So

A week or so before a person dies, you may see increased symptoms that are now more difficult to manage, related to their illness. If their condition is Heart related, you may see increased edema as the heart fails. A person dying from lung disease may experience increased shortness of breath as lung capacity diminishes. A common symptom, especially in those dying of Cancers, is increased pain. It is likely that your loved one is not eating at all at this point and therefore unable to swallow medications as well. You may have a doctor or hospice nurse suggest the implementation of sublingual (under the tongue) medications for symptom management. Some persons may benefit from a pain pump during this time.

You will notice changes in patient's Vital Signs. Blood pressure changes will occur. Sometimes blood pressure will be elevated, but more often than not, it will be low. Your loved one's heart rate will likely increase. This is occurring because the body is attempting to compensate for the decrease in function of the organs that is likely happening simultaneously. Breathing patterns will begin to change. Breathing may become more rapid or shallow. Body temperature will likely go up and down. This occurs because the brain is unable to regulate the temperature any longer. Much like when a baby is first born. This occurrence may leave the skin warm and clammy, and persons may appear pale or their skin dusky. Hands and feet may be cool to touch as circulation slows down. Just because their feet and hands are cold to you does not necessarily mean they are feeling cold. The best thing to do for this is to make sure your loved one is dressed for their comfort. That may look like them wearing their favorite hat and sweater wrapped in a blanket or it may mean they aren't dressed at all.

With more people receiving oxygen therapy at home, oxygen saturation monitors are more commonly used. As the body slows down, this oxygen-saturation monitor reading will go down. It is common for a dying person's oxygen saturation to be very low. It is in fact expected. As a hospice clinician monitoring the actual person and behaviors becomes a better gauge of what if any treatments will be implemented. I encourage the loved ones of those I've encountered on their end-of-life journey to do the same. If there is no indication to check vital signs, meaning some obvious distress, then don't. Doing so quite honestly will likely cause you distress. These numbers are no longer Vital. Blood pressure will drop; the heart rate will increase. Oxygen saturation percentage will go down and temperature will fluctuate. These are all normal occurrences. The body is doing what it was designed to do.

Another common occurrence during this time is increased "confusion" and "hallucinations." I put those in quotes because while some of those occurrences are true confusion, some are simply the ascending one's true self. The spirit. With that ascension, one is more aware spiritually of what is going on around them. During this time, your loved one may appear to be having conversations with loved ones long passed away. If this brings your loved one peace, don't intervene or try to convince them otherwise. This may cause distress. Remember the goal is comfort and peace in every aspect.

***

Days

When time has come to days before a person dies, there may be little to no communication occurring with them. At this point, your loved one is not likely taking anything by mouth. They may have brief periods of wakefulness. It is important to create a peaceful, calm environment. Meeting visitors is good. Especially those closest to the person. However, it is important not to overstimulate during this time. Even though your loved one may not be able to talk to you, they can hear you and feel your presence. I believe that these two senses are heightened as the spirit is ascending to consciousness. I often encourage loved ones of those I care for to talk to them, love on them, during this time.

Breathing patterns will continue to change. Now you may even see pauses in breathing, or gasps. This is not caused because of distress, but simply the body is slowing. Breathing pattern will continue to change until it stops. You may notice a rattle in your loved one's throat. This occurs when there is mucous pooling in the back of the throat. As muscles weaken, they aren't able to clear the mucous like they normally would. This is not believed to be painful. There are medications that can aid in drying those secretions and in some other instances, suction may be used. It is not uncommon for nothing to be done during this stage. Even those things that are implemented aren't always helpful. This is a common occurrence and is typically more uncomfortable to observe than it is for your loved one to experience.

You may notice that the skin on your loved one's feet, hands, knees, and sometimes even their back may darken during this time. Circulation is continuing to slow and therefore blood is pooling to these areas, causing the changes in skin color. Pulses may be faint at this time and their heartbeat will likely be irregular. Persons may have little to no urine or bowel movements.

If the days seem to go on longer than anticipated or your loved one appears to be transitioning but not progressing, they may be waiting. Sometimes they're waiting for the someone that they haven't seen or heard. You will know if that's the case.

***

When moving into the window of days to hours until death, what appears to be a phenomenon may occur. Persons sometimes get a burst of energy. This is what we call Rallying.

YASMEEN FATIMAH, RN

Those persons that might have been unconscious may have a sudden period of wakefulness. One that has been confused may suddenly appear to be very clear. I believe that this is also by design—similar to the burst of energy that a woman has prior to giving birth, that we call nesting; it's for preparation. An opportunity for your loved one to say things that they want to say or simply to enjoy some precious final moments before their transition. This period usually lasts a few hours. However, it's different for everyone. It could be a few minutes or what seems like an entire day. However long it last, try to be in and enjoy the moment.

***

Hours

In the last hours of life, persons may become restless. They may appear unsettled and unable to be consoled. Sometimes they are restless to the point that they can't keep still or try to get out of bed. These are all normal although uncomfortable to experience for those watching. Medication for anxiety is sometimes helpful, but sometimes not. If your loved one is receiving hospice services, they will be able to provide some support. Low light and soft music are helpful in creating a calm environment. Keeping visitor at minimum or at least ensuring that those visiting are quiet and calm will be most beneficial to your loved one. Remember they can still hear and feel presence around them.

The unrest that is experienced during birth is the spirit attaching itself to the body. The unrest that is experienced when one is dying is the spirit detaching itself from the body.

YASMEEN FATIMAH, RN

**

During this time, breathing will change. It may be more audible, especially when exhaling. Sometimes it almost sounds like a grunting. This is not caused by pain but the body adjusting to the quickly changing condition caused by the lung capacity decreasing. As the end draws near, the sound will subside and the breaths will become shallower and more spread out until they stop. At this point, eyes may be slightly opened, and the jaw typically drops some, leaving the mouth slightly opened. These are all normal occurrences.

This is obviously different for everyone. Often times loved ones want to be at the bedside and never leave during this time. Sometimes that's ok.

However, sometimes, a person won't let go while their loved ones are around. I have seen many instances where as soon as the room is empty and quiet is when the actual passing occurs. Sometimes there is one special loved one in the room, usually that one closest to the person. Where one seemed to linger for hours or even days, as soon as their surroundings were peaceful and quiet, they were able to transition.

HEAVEN STARTS HERE

*When my mother passed, of course, I knew it was coming but that did not make it much easier. Toward the end, her breathing was extremely labored, and it was hard for her to get comfortable. She was started on medication to help her rest, and that helped a lot. You don't want your loved one to "leave." But you also don't want them to suffer. We don't get to choose if they leave or not. We do get to choose in some capacity whether they suffer. I am an only child, but I was fortunate enough to be surrounded by family and friends. My mother had a friend who had been in her life for as long as I could remember. I don't know the intricate details of their relationship, being that I was a child for most of the parts that I remember. I do know that he was always around in some capacity no matter which way life took them. As my mother was transitioning, I of course let him know. I don't think he grasped how sick she was at first. So, I think he thought he had more time. She did seem to be lingering for a little while. All of my family had come, and I was at her bedside. I remember him telling me that he was on his way, so I made sure she looked pretty. I remember telling her that I was making sure that she looked pretty because he was coming. When he arrived, I left the room and gave him some time. It might have been about fifteen minutes and he came and got me. She wasn't gone but she had changed drastically. I think she was able to let go then. It seems that maybe she was waiting on him. I sat at her bedside and held her hand and told her how much I loved and appreciated her. I laid my head down on her bed and listened to her breathe her last breath.

Know that it is ok not to be ok. Even when a death is "expected," it is difficult to cope when the actual death happens. It is painful and you will need time to grieve. We don't ever get over losing a loved one. Especially those really close to us: a parent, a spouse, a sibling, or a child. We adjust to our new normal. Give yourself some grace. Remember the past is gone, tomorrow is the present in waiting, all we have is this Moment.

"The arising new heaven and by implication a new earth are not future events that are going to make us free. Nothing is going to make us free because only the present moment can make us free...Heaven is right here in the midst of you."

—*A New Earth by Eckhart Tolle*

Frequently Asked Questions

When should hospice services or other End-of-Life Care be implemented?

End-of-life care should be started as soon as the person and or the loved ones have decided that the goals of care are focused on Quality of life. The sooner these services are implemented, the better. Enlisting help early in this process allows the person and family to build a report with their nurses, aides, and/or doulas to allow for a smoother, more intimate transition.

What happens when death occurs at home?

If a person is on hospice services, the hospice will be alerted at time of death and an RN will be dispatched to do the pronouncement. Prior to this time, funeral home arrangements will have likely been made or at minimum, it is known which services will be used. The pronouncing RN will notify the funeral home, and they will come out to the home to take the deceased into their care, when the family is ready.

If the person is not on hospice, the 911 should be called. It is important that any advanced directives are available to provide to EMS at the time of arrival. Otherwise, they will be obligated to perform CPR. Once no signs of life are determined by the first responder, they will call the county coroner, who will then do the pronouncement.

Implementation of end-of-life care during this time can be very helpful in facilitating a peaceful transition and ensures ongoing bereavement support. Most hospice services and end-of-life doulas provide support for at least a year after death.

How do I obtain a death certificate?

Obtaining a death certificate is a process. It will not be available immediately. Processing time can take anywhere between two to six weeks, depending on what state you're in.

Do I contact Social Security or are they automatically notified?

It is a good idea to follow up with your local Social Security Office to be sure that they are aware of your loved one's death to avoid any over payments. They are typically already aware but it won't hurt to double check.

*Any Pensions or Retirement Entities that your loved one has been receiving payments from should also be notified as soon as possible to avoid receiving overpayments and therefore left owing moneys or decreasing any payment beneficiaries may receive.

When will I feel Better?

Grief is a process. Don't rush it. It's ok to not be ok. Take time for yourself or spend time with those you love. Do things that make you smile. If you are having a difficult time, ask for help. Losing someone close to you is an adjustment. It's not something you get over; you just adapt to a new normal.

Notes

Notes

Notes

About the Author

Yasmeen Fatimah is a registered nurse, and has specialized in hospice and palliative care for over ten years. She is a certified end of life doula (midwife), a calling that focuses on the holistic and spiritual aspect of end of life care. After recently experiencing her own spiritual awakening, she has realized that she is an Earth Angel. She possesses a special connection to the Divine, with a knowing that allows her to speak directly to the souls of those embarking on this journey, helping them to gain clarity, and serving as a bridge to the unknown.

Yasmeen was born and raised in Atlanta, Georgia, and is now the mother of four amazing human beings. She had the privilege of living in Hawaii on the island of Oahu for almost ten years. That is where she discovered a love for the ocean and all its wonder, and how peaceful the water really is. On her journey she realized why her love for the water is so vast. Water is the most powerful element because it is perfectly nonresistant. In that same spirit, she has learned simply to be, and to allow things to flow like water. She believes we must make space for all things to work together as they should, and allow ourselves to be in the moment and soak it in. For, truly, the moment is all we have.

For Information on End of Life Care,
Support and Resources Contact

earthangelshpc@gmail.com

www.ingramcontent.com/pod-product-compliance
Lightning Source LLC
LaVergne TN
LVHW051926060526
838201LV00062B/4703